HELEN KELLER

Richard Tames

FRANKLIN WATTS
LONDON•SYDNEY

Contents

This edition 2003

Franklin Watts
96 Leonard Street
London
EC2A 4XD

Franklin Watts Australia
45-51 Huntley Street
Alexandria, NSW 2015

© Franklin Watts 1989, 2003

Series Editor: Penny Horton
Designer: Ross George

A CIP catalogue record for this book is
available from the British Library.

ISBN 0 7496 5024 9

Printed in Belgium

Into Darkness

Helen Keller was born in the small country town of Tuscumbia, Alabama on 27 June 1880. Her father was a newspaper editor turned United States Marshal. He had fought in the American Civil War (1861–5) and kept his military title of Captain. Helen's mother was a lady of charm and grace who came from a wealthy family. The Kellers were not, themselves, a wealthy family, but they lived comfortably in a pleasant house at the end of a shady lane.

In February 1882 baby Helen fell ill. She had a fever and was in great pain, but the doctor did not know what was wrong with her. At last the terrible illness passed. The pain and the fever went. But, so too did Helen's sight and hearing. The mysterious illness left her both blind and deaf.

Shut up in a world of silence and darkness, Helen sometimes acted more like an angry animal than a little girl. Unable to see, hear or speak, she would hit or kick at anything or anyone within her reach. She could cry. She could scream. But she could not talk.

However, Helen could still smell and touch things. She could follow her mother around by clutching on to her skirt. She liked to get to know people by running her fingers over their faces and clothes. She also came to understand that people

At the end of a shady lane — the Keller's home in Tuscumbia, Alabama.

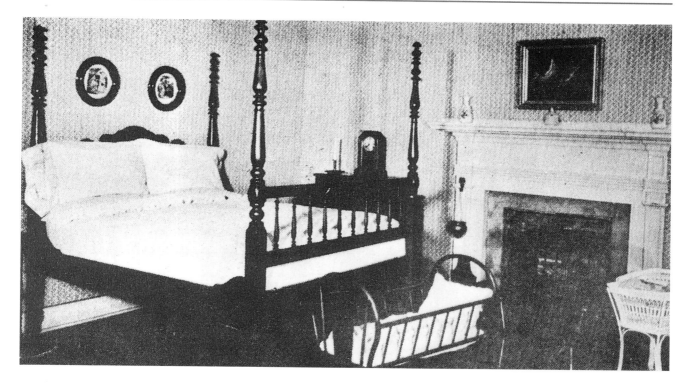

Above: **A comfortable home – the room where Helen Keller was born.**

talked to one another. She could feel people's lips move and feel the vibrations in their throats as they made the noises of speech. Helen wanted to join in, so she cried or screamed with anger. Years later Helen remembered:-

"I broke dishes and lamps ... I put my hands into everybody's plates ... I came into the parlour in my red flannel underwear and pinched Grandma ... chasing her from the room."

Naturally, people in Tuscumbia had their own opinions about this unusual child. One of her uncles thought she ought to be locked away because she was so naughty, but an aunt thought that she could be a clever little girl – if only she could

Captain Arthur Keller – soldier, newspaperman and US Marshal.

find some way to express herself.

Helen did find a way of making up her own sign language. To refer to her father, she pretended to put on imaginary glasses. To refer to her mother she pretended to tie up her hair. And if she wanted ice cream she would shiver. In all she made up over 60 different signs for people or things. She also learned to help out with household chores – folding laundry, milking the cows and making pastry.

Helen's father decided to write to Dr Alexander Graham Bell, who lived in Washington and was famous as the inventor of the telephone. Dr Bell's wife and mother were both deaf and he was very interested in

Helen and Lioness. The death of her constant companion started Helen on her career of helping others.

the problems of deaf people. He advised Captain Keller to get in touch with Michael Anagnos, the director of the Perkins Institution for the Blind in Boston, Massachusetts. Mr Anagnos replied to his letter at once:-

"The case of your little daughter is of exceeding interest to me. Your brief description of her mental activity reminds me of Laura Bridgman … ".

Mr Anagnos said he would try to find a suitable teacher for Helen. He did. Her name was Annie Sullivan.

The Bell Telephone

Alexander Graham Bell (1847–1922) was born in Scotland but **emigrated** to Canada in 1870, and from there to the United States in 1871 where he became a professor at Boston University in 1873. His special interest lay in experimenting with the problems of speech, sound and hearing. He also spent much time teaching the system of "visible speech" for the deaf, invented by his father, Alexander Melville Bell, and helped found an association for the teaching of speech to the deaf. In 1876 he filed a **patent** for a telephone. An American engineer, Elisha Gray, filed a patent on the very same day, 14 February, but Bell beat him by hours to be recognized as the authorized inventor. Later that year Bell gave a public demonstration of his new invention to celebrate the first 100 years of American independence.

In 1877 he saw the telephone used in business for the first time. He went on to establish the highly successful Bell Telephone Company and to reap the full rewards of his **ingenuity.** When he died the whole American telephone system observed a one minute silence in tribute.

Alexander Graham Bell giving a public demonstration of his revolutionary invention – the telephone.

Annie and Helen

Unlike Helen Keller, Annie Sullivan was not born into a comfortable home with doting parents. Her mother and father had fled from a great **famine** in Ireland and settled near the industrial town of Springfield, Massachusetts. When Annie was five she began to suffer from an eye disease, **trachoma,** which gradually made her sight worse.

When Annie was eight her mother died and, after living with relatives, Annie was sent to live in a poorhouse with 900 other people.

Annie could not see well enough to read herself and had never been to school, but when she heard that there were special schools for the blind she decided she wanted to go to one more than anything else in the world. In 1880, at the age of 14, she got her chance and was transferred to the Perkins Institution for the Blind in the bustling city of Boston.

Annie was unhappy at Perkins. The other girls laughed at her because they thought she was poor, ignorant and ill-mannered. But Annie soon showed that she had a mind of her own. She shocked the other girls by arguing with her teachers and the school's director, Mr Anagnos.

Two operations at a Catholic charity hospital dramatically improved Annie's sight so that she could read. Annie made friends with Laura Bridgman, the deaf-blind woman who had lived at Perkins for over 40 years.

Annie graduated from Perkins when she was 20 and left at the top of her class. One year later Michael

Left: **It was not long before Helen came to love Annie as her teacher and friend.**

Above: **Laura Bridgman.**

Left: **The cottage in
the garden where
Helen and Annie made
a new beginning.**

Anagnos wrote to Captain Keller about Annie:

"She is exceedingly intelligent, strictly honest, **industrious,** ladylike in her manner ... She is familiar with Laura Bridgman's case and with the methods of teaching deaf, mute and blind children, and I assure you she will make an excellent instructress and most reliable guide for your little daughter."

It was more than 2280 kilometres (1800 miles) from Boston to Alabama and the journey took several days. When Annie at last arrived at the Keller's house she was tired as well as nervous. Her first meeting with Helen was upsetting:-

"I remember how disappointed I was when the untamed little creature stubbornly refused to kiss me and struggled to free herself from my embrace."

Annie soon found out that Helen had a quick temper and a good deal of **obstinacy,** but knew how to handle her, as she wrote to a friend:-

"The greatest problem I shall have to solve is how to discipline and control her without breaking her spirit. I shall go rather slowly at first and try to win her love. I shall not attempt to conquer her by force alone; but I shall insist on reasonable obedience from the start."

Annie decided that the most practical thing to do would be to live with Helen in a little garden cottage, quite apart from the main house. Helen continued to have temper tantrums but also, slowly came to understand that no one was going to interfere when Annie wanted her to do something. It took a week for Annie to tame Helen. Then the learning could really begin.

Left: **Entering a new world – Helen reading from a Braille book.**

"I spell in her hand everything we do all day long, although she has no idea yet what the spelling means."

One day, as Helen remembered many years later, a little miracle happened. Annie and Helen were out for a walk when Annie saw someone pumping water. Annie led Helen over to the pump and put her hand under the spout:-

" ... as the cool stream gushed over one hand, she spelled into the other the word water ... I stood still, my whole attention fixed upon the motions of her fingers ... I knew then that W-A-T-E-R meant the wonderful cool something that was flowing over my hand ... As we returned to the house every object which I touched seemed to quiver with life."

Annie realized then:-

" ... that the education of this child will be the distinguishing event of my life if I have the brains and **perseverance** to accomplish it."

After four months with Annie, Helen knew 300 words and could count up to 30. She was also about to write her first letter, using a special writing board, with grooves cut in it. Paper was placed over the board and Helen used the forefinger of her left hand to guide the pencil point along the grooves so that the letters she wrote came out neatly next to one another and made proper words.

By the end of six months Helen knew almost another 300 words and her five times table. She had also mastered Braille.

When Annie told Helen that there were little blind girls like herself at the Perkins Institution in faraway Boston, Helen decided to write them a letter:-

"Helen and teacher will come to see little blind girls. Helen and teacher will go in steam car to Boston. Helen and blind girls will have fun blind girls can talk on fingers."

Great Hunger in Ireland 1845–7

Annie Sullivan grew up in the United States because her family had come there to escape the great famine in Ireland. Ireland's population of four million lived almost entirely on a diet of potatoes. When potato crops became diseased, destroying the harvest in 1845 and in 1846 the result was a catastrophe. Almost a million people died of starvation or disease. Many people felt that their only chance of a decent life was to flee the country. Between 1847 and 1861, over two million Irish people crossed the Atlantic Ocean to the hope of a better life in the United States. Some found it. Others, like Annie Sullivan's family did not.

A crowd of starving people, desperate to enter a workhouse for food and shelter during the potato famine in Ireland.

Going Away

Above: **Helen with Michael Agagnos.**

Left: **The big city, Boston, a new experience for Helen.**

Annie realized that Helen was an exceptionally gifted child. This meant that she had to make herself a better teacher to enable Helen to make the most of her abilities. She wanted to ask Mr Anagnos for his advice and she needed to buy special equipment and Braille books for Helen. She also wanted to get away from Alabama. She knew that local people disliked her as a "Yankee".

In the summer of 1888 Helen, aged eight, set out for Boston with her mother and "Teacher" as she now called Annie. Helen had already become quite famous and on the way they stopped in Washington, where they met President Cleveland at the White House. Helen also met the inventor, Dr Alexander Graham Bell, who had put her father in touch with Mr Anagnos two years before.

Helen and Dr Bell liked each other at once and became good friends.

When they got to Boston, Helen and Teacher went to stay with Mr Anagnos. Helen did not join as a pupil at Perkins. She thought Helen learned best by actually doing things. So Helen learned history by visiting places where famous events had happened. And she found out what the sea was by being knocked over by a wave!

Helen liked being with the blind girls at Perkins because they "talked" to her with the manual alphabet. But she also liked being back home in Tuscumbia, where she could ride her pony, Black Beauty, and play with her dog, Lioness. She also loved the countryside, where there were so many new and interesting plants to touch and smell.

Helen was completely deaf but she could feel vibrations. So she could "hear" Lioness barking by putting her fingers around the dog's throat. And she could beat time to music by putting her hands on a piano when it was being played. When she learned that a blind-deaf girl in Norway had learned to speak Helen decided that she had to learn as well. A teacher called Miss Fuller was found and began to show Helen how sounds were made by putting Helen's fingers inside her mouth to feel how the tongue and lips moved to produce each sound. After ten lessons Helen said her first sentence:- "It is warm."

Helen became a friendly and generous child. When she learned that a little blind-deaf boy called Tommy Stringer was too poor to go to a special school she was very upset. Soon afterwards her pet dog Lioness wandered into town alone, and because there was a very strict local law against dogs which were not on a lead a policeman shot Lioness dead. The man who gave Lioness to Helen sent a letter which she had written to him to a newspaper, which printed it. People as far away as England heard about the little blind-deaf girl who had lost her pet. Money poured in from people who wanted her to have another dog. Helen wrote and thanked them but said she wanted to use the money to help Tommy Stringer. A special fund was set up and soon there was enough money to send Tommy to Perkins. Helen had begun to show how much she could care for others. But she was also aware of the limits of her own powers and declared simply, "I do not know what I should do without Teacher."

Helen's letters were the saving of Tommy Stringer. But the following year, 1891, it was her story writing that got her into trouble. Annie had told Helen about the wonderful colours of the trees in autumn. So Helen made up a story about how King Frost put the colours on the

Helen (left) and schoolfriends. The little boy is Tommy Stringer, whose school fees were paid from funds raised by Helen's personal appeal.

leaves to make people less sad about the end of summer. Helen sent a copy of *The Frost King* to Mr Anagnos as a birthday present. He thought it was so good that he had it printed. Helen suddenly became a famous writer.

But only a week or so after *The Frost King* appeared some of its readers noticed that it was very much like a story called *The Frost Fairies* which had been written a few years before. Helen and Annie were called cheats. Mr Anagnos was furious and spent hours questioning Annie and Helen. It seems that Annie had never heard of *The Frost Fairies*. But a friend of hers had read it to Helen, who stored it away in her amazing memory. When Annie had started to tell Helen about the autumn leaves she must have remembered the story and written it down in her own words, believing it to be her own idea. Sadly, it caused the end of the friendship between Mr Anagnos, and Helen and Annie.

But another friend helped to cheer them up. Dr Bell arranged a surprise holiday for them at Niagara Falls. Annie described the great walls of water as vividly as ever and Helen could feel the vibrations of their power and the fine mist they threw off. Dr Bell then took them on to the **World's Fair** at Chicago for three weeks. Helen had a wonderful time touching all the exhibits. And everywhere she went crowds gathered round to see her. Helen Keller was becoming quite as famous as any exhibit at the fair.

At Niagara, with Dr Bell and Helen's mother, Annie described the falls to Helen as she felt their spray.

Helen was now becoming a young woman. Although she continued to call Annie "Teacher" she noticed a change between them:- "She ceased to treat me as a child. She did not command me any more." Annie and Helen had become true friends.

From Scholar to Speaker

In 1894 Helen and Annie entered the Wright-Humason School in New York, where deaf people were taught to speak. Helen amazed the other children, who were deaf but sighted, when she showed them how she could read chalk writing on a blackboard with her fingers. She also showed them that she could play chess – and win. Apart from training her voice and learning to read a speaker's lips with her fingers, Helen also began to learn German. Annie continued to take her on interesting trips and to meet famous people. On one occasion Helen met the writer Mark Twain, who became a great admirer of hers and wrote:-

Helen with America's foremost man of letters – Mark Twain.

"You are a wonderful creature, the most wonderful in the world … you and your other half together – Miss Sullivan, I mean, for it took the pair of you to make a complete and perfect whole."

Helen thoroughly enjoyed learning and decided to go to university. Few ordinary girls had more than a school education in those days. For a blind-deaf girl to achieve this was truly remarkable.

When she was 16 Helen entered the Cambridge School for Young Ladies in Massachusetts. She had been to a school where all the pupils were blind and to a school where all the pupils were deaf. Now she was at a school where no one was blind or deaf. She joined classes in French, Latin, German, English, Greek, Roman History and mathematics. Later she added physics, geometry and **astronomy**. She would have to work very hard to keep up, and Annie would have to work even harder to help her.

When Helen went to a lecture Annie would have to spell into her hand everything that was being said. Annie also had to read almost all her study books for her and then pass on the information as so few books she needed had ever been printed in Braille. Sometimes the strain would show and they would argue with each other. Finally,

Above: **Serene scholarship – Helen reading by herself in 1899.**

Above left: **A restful moment in a life devoted to study.**

Helen fell ill. The principal of Cambridge School thought that they ought to be separated. For a short while they were, but their many good friends saw that Helen could not manage without Annie and that Annie was miserable without Helen. Soon they were together again. But the Principal of Cambridge would not take them back. Even so, in 1899 Helen passed the entrance examination for Radcliffe College, the women's section of Harvard University.

At Radcliffe Helen was very popular. But she did not have much spare time for sport or social occasions. She had to work even harder to keep up with the others. And so, of course, did Annie. In the end Helen took 17 courses of study, ranging from the Bible to Shakespeare, from **economics** to **philosophy**.

When it came to taking her final examinations, Annie was sent away and a university official spelled the questions into Helen's hand. Helen typed her answers out so perfectly that they were given a place of honour in the university's museum. They also won her the degree of Bachelor of Arts with Honours.

Braille

The Braille system was devised by Louis Braille (1809–1852) a French teacher, who was himself blinded by an accident at the age of three. Braille realized that, rather than teach blind people how to work out raised versions of the standard roman alphabet, it would be more efficient to design a system which was actually intended to be "read" by touch. He invented a method of creating raised dots on paper in combinations to stand for different sounds. The dots are punched on to the paper to make them stand out, so that people can feel the dots, enabling them to "read" with their hands. A modern Braille code for the English language was finally completed in 1932. Each of the 63 characters consists of from one to six dots.

Reading Braille. The very first Braille book was published in French in 1829 but there were none available in English before 1870.

17

Success

" ... two teachers instead of one." – Helen with John Macy and Annie. But the partnership was not to last as John and Annie drifted apart.

Busy as she was, Helen also found time to keep up her own personal interest in writing. In 1893 she had written a short account of her life, which was published in a magazine for young people. Many people wanted to know more about her and in 1901 she agreed to write about herself for the *Ladies Home Journal*. Helen and Annie were helped by an experienced writer and publisher called John Macy. Between them they produced a three part book which was published in 1903 as *The Story of My Life*. The first part was Helen's account of her own life, the second was a selection of her letters and the third a description of her education written by John Macy.

The Story of My Life was an enormous success. Helen and Annie suddenly became rich. They no longer had to rely on the kind generosity of friends. They could afford to buy expensive clothes and travel in style. They bought a big house with large grounds. John Macy continued to spend a lot of time with them and in 1905 he married Annie. Helen was not jealous but wrote:-

"Think of my happiness. I am to have two teachers instead of one."

Helen was now secure in her own home. She was free from the pressure of study. True to her character she became intensely interested in what was going on in the world and what she could do about the aspects of society and politics that troubled her. Ever since she had helped little Tommy Stringer get to Perkins she had cared about other people. Now she had the freedom and confidence to start doing what she could for them. In 1905 she took up her first public appointment as a member of the Massachusetts Commission for the Blind.

All her life Helen Keller had had to struggle to succeed and she had succeeded brilliantly. Now she took up the cause of people who had to struggle to survive. People living in slums, children who were forced to go out to work, black people who were unable to get decent jobs or homes.

Helen also supported other causes that were unpopular in the United States at that time, such as birth control and the ending of **capital punishment**. Helen had a particular sympathy for women – women who were trying to bring up their children in damp and dirty houses; women who were on strike for better wages; women who demanded the right to vote. Helen's family and friends thought her opinions were very extreme but they could not shake her from her cause and in 1913 she published a book of essays on socialism called *Out of the Dark*.

By 1914 Helen had worked so hard on her speech that she could talk at public meetings. She went on a lecture tour and attracted massive crowds. In the same year war broke out in Europe. Helen spoke out strongly against the United States getting involved. 1914 also brought personal tragedy to Annie. John Macy's work and his interest in socialist politics kept him away from home more and more. Annie became overweight and was often ill. Finally, John left her altogether and at the same time the money ran out. Helen and Annie would have to go and give lectures not only to tell their wonderful story but because they needed the money.

Speaking out – the press saw Helen as a unique expert on blindness.

Below: **Public lecturing enabled Helen to reach a far wider audience.**

Socialism

The growth of modern industry in Europe and North America created extremes of wealth and poverty, especially in the great cities where the contrast between rich and poor was most obvious. Socialists argued that the power to create wealth through industry should be controlled by the government for the benefit of all, rather than by individuals for their own advantage. People against socialism argued that governments would always be less efficient in creating wealth than individuals.

Socialism has always had more followers in Europe than in North America. Helen and John Macy were definitely backing an unpopular cause when they announced that they were socialists.

A line-up of men, queuing for food, New York, 1888. Socialists were angered by the existence of poverty in a world capable of producing plenty.

On the Move

Above: **Polly Thomson – Annie's successor – who began as Helen's hairdresser and housekeeper.**

Lecturing took Helen and Annie all over the United States. To help them make all the complicated arrangements for travel and hotels and lecture halls they took on Polly Thomson, a young girl from Scotland. She also became Helen's hairdresser and housekeeper. Polly became an expert at the manual alphabet and was able to "talk" to Helen very quickly.

Helen's lecture tour was such a success that she had to employ another secretary to help her with all the letters she received. His name was Peter Fagan and after a short time working together, he told her that he wanted to marry her. Helen's mother found out that Helen and Peter planned to run away together and leave Annie behind. She was so angry that when Peter came to the Keller house in Tuscumbia he was sent away at gun point. He never came back.

When Annie regained her health, she and Helen and Polly went back to lecturing. Then, in 1918, a studio in Hollywood offered to make a film about Helen's life. It was a wonderful opportunity. Helen could earn the money she needed so badly and at the same time give a message of hope to other people who were disabled or poor or had unhappy lives. The film was to be called *Deliverance*. The posters advertised Helen as "the eighth wonder of the world".

Below: **A poster advertising Helen's first and only film.**

Helen met famous film stars like Charlie Chaplin and acted the part of herself in the film. Unfortunately, it was not a great success and so Helen and Annie still needed to make money. As a result, they decided to tell their story themselves, on the stage. Annie and Helen worked out an act and toured the variety theatres which presented comedians, dancers, animal acts and conjurors. Annie would tell how she met Helen. Then they would act out Helen's discovery of W-A-T-E-R, and finally, Helen would answer questions from the audience.

In 1921 an American Foundation for the Blind was established to set up more schools for the blind and to produce more and better books in Braille. In 1924 Helen, Annie and Polly began to work for the Foundation, giving lectures to raise money.

For three years they toured the United States. Helen visited over 100 cities and talked to more than 250,000 people.

In 1927 the touring stopped and Helen returned to writing again. She published a book called *My Religion* which explained how she had been influenced by the ideas of Emanuel Swedenborg (1688-1772) who argued that logic and science proved the existence of God. In 1929 Helen published *Midstream: My Later Life,* which brought her biography up to date.

Annie tried to help Helen with her writing but her eyesight was beginning to fail. Polly began to take over more and more of this work, helped by a publisher, Nella Braddy Henney. In the end, Annie had to have one of her eyes removed. With the other she could see only one tenth of

Helen (centre) on her vaudeville tour. Note the flowers – a constant delight throughout her life.

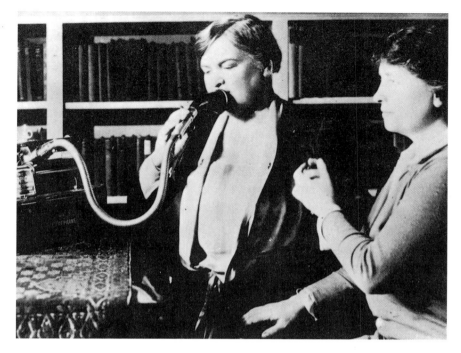

Left: **Annie, using a dictaphone to take dictation from Helen, shows technology helping the disabled.**

Below: **Helen** (left) **and Polly on holiday in Scotland. Annie's absence suggests how much Polly was taking over from her.**

normal vision.

In 1931 and 1932 Helen, Annie and Polly travelled through Europe. They went to the United Kingdom where they visited Polly's family in Scotland and met the King and Queen at Buckingham Palace. They visited Ireland and went on to France and Yugoslavia, as the personal guests of the King.

When she returned to the United States Helen took the lead in organizing a World Conference for the Blind. Helen and Annie went back to England and Scotland in 1933. In the same year Annie's life story, written by Nella, was published. Annie's sight got worse and worse, until she was almost blind. In October 1936 she had an operation on her remaining eye. It was unsuccessful and the strain of the operation led to her death shortly afterwards. Helen had lost her true friend and teacher.

President Roosevelt

Franklin Delano Roosevelt (1882–1945) was born into a wealthy and influential family and rose rapidly in politics to become a United States senator before he was 30. In 1921 he was crippled by **polio** but refused to give up public life and went on to become President in 1932.

Helen Keller had already begun to try to influence him and saw the results of her efforts in 1935 when a new Social Security Act was passed by Congress which enabled taxes to be used to help the blind. In the same year, government money was used for the first time to fund 5,000 "talking book" record players for the blind.

In 1938 Helen persuaded President Roosevelt to set up a special committee to buy products made by the blind, such as mats, mops, brooms and mattresses, for use in government offices, prisons and hospitals. President Roosevelt recognized the power of Helen's influence and declared, "Anything Helen Keller is for, I am for."

President Roosevelt, himself confined to a wheelchair, had a direct understanding from his own experience of the problems of the disabled.

War and Its Price

Helen's diaries show that she missed "Teacher" almost every day. But she was determined to keep on with her work for other blind people and Polly took up the task of supporting her where Annie had left off. In 1937 they made a tour of Japan. It was a huge success. They travelled to 39 cities and were received by the Emperor and Empress. As a result of this tour, the Japanese government agreed to set up new ways of helping handicapped people.

In 1939, World War II broke out in Europe. Helen was against American involvement as she had been 25 years before during World War I. But she changed her mind as she learned more about the evil of Hitler and the Nazis. In Vienna they closed down the Jewish Institute and turned its blind students out on to

Above: **Helen and Polly dressed in traditional silk kimono celebrate their Japanese tour.**

Left: **The attack on Pearl Harbor, 7 December 1941, which brought the United States into World War II.**

the streets to beg or starve. When the Japanese attacked the United States base at Pearl Harbor, Helen became convinced that the United States had no option but to fight and she wanted to play her part.

Wars produce casualties – wounded men who are often disabled or even blinded. Helen made it her special mission to visit them in hospital. They knew how hard she had had to struggle to overcome her handicaps and many of them had read about her in their text books when they were at school. Now she was standing beside them. Helen realized perhaps better than many that:-

"They do not want to be treated as heroes. They want to be able to live naturally and to be treated as human beings."

The atomic bombing of Nagasaki by the United States in August 1945.

Helen called her visits to the wounded, "the crowning experience of my life."

When the war ended Helen toured shattered Europe, visiting Greece, Italy, France and England. While she was away she heard that the house at Arcan Ridge, built for her by the American Foundation for the Blind, had burned down. With it she had lost her books, her diaries, her letters and press cuttings and, perhaps worst of all, the manuscript of the book she was writing about Annie. But when she thought of the devastation around her in Europe it did not seem such a crushing blow.

Later Helen went back to Japan. In Hiroshima and Nagasaki she met people who had been horribly burned by the blast from the atomic bombs. She felt their dreadful scars and vowed to campaign against the production and use of such weapons.

Above: **Helen dancing with a blinded soldier who lost his sight in the War.**

World in Despair

The collapse of world trade between 1929 and 1931 led to mass unemployment. Desperate voters in different countries gave their support to new leaders. In the United States this meant President Roosevelt and his "New Deal" policies which were designed to create jobs by using taxes to build dams and plant forests. In Germany and Japan it meant giving power to leaders who used taxes to build up their armed forces. In 1937 Japan attacked China and in 1939 Germany attacked Poland. The United States stayed out of the war until December 1941 when the Japanese made a surprise attack on the United States naval base at Pearl Harbor, Hawaii.

American troops fought in both Europe and Africa against Germany and Italy and in the Pacific Ocean against Japan. President Roosevelt guided the United States through the war until his sudden death in April 1945, a few weeks before the final defeat of Germany. In August 1945 American aeroplanes dropped atomic bombs on the cities of Hiroshima and Nagasaki. Japan surrendered a few days later.

Unemployed men line up patiently for free food rations in New York's Times Square – heart of a once prosperous city.

Ever Onward

Left: **"Namas te."**
Helen makes a
traditional Hindu
greeting to India's
Prime Minister Nehru.

Below: **Helen and Polly**
at a restaurant,
enjoying their later
years together.

In 1948 Polly Thomson suffered a stroke. But Helen's energy seemed as boundless as it had ever been. In 1951 she visited South Africa and the following year went to five countries in the Middle East. In 1953 she toured Latin America. In the same year a new film about her life was released. It was called *The Unconquered* and won an Academy Award.

In 1955 Helen finally published her own account of Annie's life and work. It was called simply *Teacher*. The same year saw her visit India, return to Japan and become the first woman ever to be awarded an honorary degree by Harvard University.

In 1957 a play about Helen, *The Miracle Worker,* performed its first production. It was a great success and became a prize-winning film.

Helen was now nearly 80 years old. Her senses of smell and touch, on which she relied so much, were beginning to fade. Polly was also losing her health and becoming very difficult to live with. For the last two years of her life she was an invalid. Polly finally died in 1960.

Helen's eightieth birthday was an occasion for many tributes. Leading newspapers reviewed her life's achievements. When a reporter from the Herald Tribune asked her about her plans for the future she replied:-

"I will always – as long as I have breath – work for the handicapped."

At her birthday luncheon, Helen presented the first Helen Keller International Award to the blind Colonel Baker, head of the Canadian Institute for the Blind. Then she went back to her old college, Radcliffe, to dedicate the Anne Sullivan Memorial Fountain, which was set in a garden of beautiful flowers. Helen smelled the flowers and said just one word, "WATER".

After Polly's death, Helen made few public appearances. Like Polly, she suffered several strokes and gradually lost the power to think and communicate clearly. But she was lovingly cared for until her death in 1968.

Helen Keller herself summed up her life when she wrote:-

"I have always looked upon the blind as part of the whole society, and my desire has been to help them regain their human rights so as to enable them to keep a place of usefulness and dignity in the world … What I say of the blind applies equally to all hindered groups … ".

Few human beings have ever been as hindered as Helen Keller or travelled as far and achieved so much.

Below right: **A message of hope – Helen spells out her personal philosophy.**

Below: **A monument to Annie Sullivan symbolizes her role in Helen's life.**

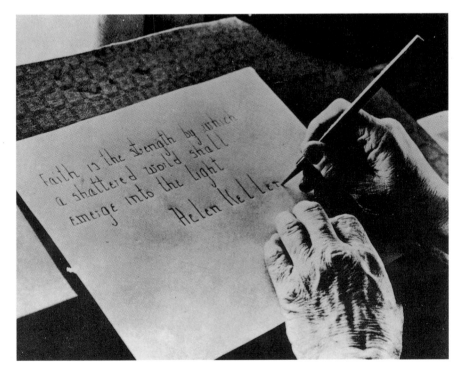

Find out More ...

Important Dates

1845-7 "Great Hunger" in Ireland
1861-6 Civil War in America
1866 Birth of Annie Sullivan
1876 Alexander Graham Bell
demonstrates his telephone
1880 Birth of Helen Keller
1882 Helen loses her sight and
hearing
1887 Annie meets Helen
1888 Helen visits Boston
1891 *The Frost King*
1894 Helen attends the Wright-
Humason School
1900 Helen enters Radcliffe
1903 *The Story of My Life*
1905 Annie marries John Macy
1909 Helen becomes a socialist

1913 *Out of the Dark*
1914 Polly Thomson joins Helen
and Annie
1919 *Deliverance*
1924 Helen works for the
American Foundation for
the Blind
1936 Death of "Teacher"
1937 Helen visits Japan
1943 Helen visits the wounded
1946 Helen tours Europe
1953 *The Unconquered*
1955 *Teacher*
1957 *The Miracle Worker*
1960 Death of Polly Thomson
1961 Helen retires from public life
1968 Death of Helen Keller

Useful Information

**Helen Keller National Center for
Deaf-Blind Youths and Adults**
111 Middle Neck Road
Sands Point
New York, NY 11050
USA
www.helenkeller.org

Helen Keller Worldwide
352 Park Avenue South
12th Floor
New York, NY 10010
USA
www.hkworld.org

Perkins School for the Blind
175 North Beacon Street
Watertown, Massachusetts 02472
USA
www.perkins.pvt.k12.ma.us

**Royal National Institute
for the Blind, UK**
PO Box 173
Peterborough
PE2 6WS
*www.rnib.org.uk/wesupply/
fctsheet/keller.htm*

**The Helen Keller Foundation for
Research and Education**
1201 11th Avenue South, Suite 300
Birmingham, Alabama 35205
USA
www.helenkellerfoundation.org

Glossary

Astronomy   The study of the stars and planets.

Capital Punishment   To be sentenced to death, for serious crime, such as murder.

Economics   The study of how people and communities meet their needs for goods and services through production and trade.

Emigrated   Gone to live in another country to make it one's home.

Famine   Widespread hunger in a community, usually the result of harvest failure.

Industrious   Hard-working.

Ingenuity   The ability to find clever ways of solving a problem.

Obstinacy   Persistent refusal to change an action or attitude.

Patent   A legal document giving an inventor the right to stop other people copying his or her invention without permission.

Perseverance   Sticking to a task, despite any difficulties.

Philosophy   The study of the writings of wise men and women about the problems and meaning of human life.

Polio   A disease of the spine which often results in crippling of the arms or legs; nowadays, this disease is usually only found in developing countries.

Trachoma   An infectious disease of the eyes, resulting in damage or loss of sight; nowadays, the disease is usually only found in developing countries.

World's Fair   A giant exhibition, showing unusual and interesting objects from many countries.

Index

Picture Acknowledgements

The publishers would like to thank the following for their kind permission to reproduce their photographs in this book:
The American Foundation for the Blind Cover, frontispiece, 4,5 (top), 9 (left), 16 (right), 18,19 (left), 21 (top), 22,23 (bottom), 25 (top), 26 (bottom), 28 (top & bottom), 30; New York Public Library 5 (bottom), 6,15,29 (left & right); The Perkins School for the Blind 9 (left & right), 10,12 (right), 13,14,19 (right), 21 (bottom), 23 (top). Photographer: Paul Seheult. The Royal National Institute for the Blind 16 (left), 17.
The following photographs were supplied by: BBC Hulton Picture Library 7,11,12 (left), 20,24,25 (bottom), 26 (top), 27.

PRINTED IN BELGIUM BY proost INTERNATIONAL BOOK PRODUCTION